ANIMALS
AT MY
DOORSTEP

BY

HELEN HOOVER

Illustrated by SYMEON SHIMIN

Parents' Magazine Press • New York

My Cabin in the Woods

The log cabin where I live is in the midst of a very large forest that reaches for miles and miles across northern Minnesota and far into Canada. When I look out of the window by my desk, I see trees, and beyond them, a beautiful lake.

When I go outside, I walk through a little clear space where the trees have been cut down so that the sunlight can reach the cabin. The clearing is green with tall grass and ferns in summer, and has purple violets and white daisies and blue asters and golden dandelions scattered around for trimming. In winter it is all white with deep snow, and only the tracks of my animal friends break the smoothness.

All around the clearing stand the trees that make up the forest, young ones as small as Christmas trees, ancient ones as tall as ten-story buildings. In summer the breeze brings me the scent of pine and damp earth, and in winter the air is so fresh and cold that it makes my nose crinkle inside.

When I first came here to live I did not see

many of the forest creatures except as quick movements as they scurried to hide from me. The only way to show them that I was friendly was with food. So I began to put out crumbs and grain, and I hung feeders full of suet from the trees.

My wild neighbors began to come to eat—red squirrels and blue jays, tiny chickadees and big deer, even a white ermine with a pink nose and a black tailtip. Soon they learned that I would not hurt them. My wild neighbors became my animal friends, and I learned something very wonderful—everything that grows and lives is important to all the other things.

A squirrel runs through the grass and a fuzzy seed sticks to his fur. Somewhere it falls off and a new plant grows. A chipmunk comes along and eats some of the plant's leaves. Then the plant bears seeds and two deer mice begin to nibble them. An ermine catches one of the mice for dinner. The other mouse makes a nest of grass and moss, and stores many seeds there for winter food. He does not eat them all and those that are left sprout in the spring.

A snowshoe hare brings her large family to feed there. They would soon eat all the young green plants, but an owl catches one and a fox another, so that there are no longer too many hares. Some of the green things are left to grow tall. Their branches shade my window and soon bend under the weight of bunches of red berries for robins to eat.

It gets warm and rainy and there are mosquitoes everywhere. Birds eat some of them and a hawk swoops out of the sky to catch one of the birds. Some of the mosquitoes eat plant juice. As they fly from one plant to another, they brush against the flowers and carry the golden dust called pollen from one flower to another. This helps the plants make seeds to sprout the following spring. When it grows cold and the snow falls, the graceful deer come out of the shadows under the trees to eat twigs from the bushes that shaded my window and fed the robins in summer.

So the forest life goes on. All the wild creatures work together so that there are the right number of every kind, and enough food for everyone.

It would take a very large book to tell you about the hundreds and hundreds of different living things in my forest, so I will tell you about several of them that I know especially well. Most of these even come to visit right at my doorstep.

Animal Camouflage

A soft, white bunny, called a showshoe hare, is hopping across the soft, white snow in my woods. His fur coat looks just like the snow. When he sits down and does not move, I can hardly see him. Nature has *camouflaged* him. This means that he is dressed up to look like something else so that his enemies cannot see and catch him.

When the snow begins to melt and look dirty, the bunny begins to change his white coat for a brown one, hair by hair. Soon his fur will be the color of the dirty snow. A little later, his coat will be made up of brown and white patches. This coat will match the ground, where little patches of earth show through the white, partly melted snow. Then, when the snow is all gone, he will be dressed in neat brown, the color of the earth and of the shadows under the leaves.

My pet ermine also wears a white coat in winter

and a brown one in summer, and some animals, like frogs, toads, fish, and lizards, can change color at any time to match things around them.

Last summer, on a gray log beside my bed of purple pansies I saw a bright orange butterfly. When I looked again, it had disappeared. I thought it had flown away but, as I watched, it opened its wings. Only the top side of the wings was brightly colored. The underside, which was all I could see when the butterfly closed its wings, was gray and looked exactly like the bark of the log.

The end of the log was covered with moss like green velvet. I saw a piece of the moss start to walk away—but it wasn't moss. It was a green spider that matched the moss perfectly.

A little strip of birch bark lay on the log. I picked it up—and it wiggled! It was a caterpillar, dressed to look like bark. This reminded me of other insects I have seen, or rather, almost didn't see, because they looked so much like something else...the walking stick who looks just like a dead twig when he stands still, the green katydid, hidden in the green leaves of trees, and the cabbage worm that is the exact blue-green color as the plants he feeds upon.

I walked into the forest, where rays of light reached down past the high branches of the tall trees. I came to a sheltered hollow, where the sunbeams fell through the leaves of a bush to spatter the brown, fallen pine needles with shimmering drops of light. As I watched, the spotted earth seemed to move a little and I saw a fawn lying there. The white spots on her brown coat were so like the sun drops on the needles that I should not have seen her if she had not moved.

Her slim legs were folded close to her body and her tail was neatly tucked in. She was small enough for you to hold on your lap and her four tiny hoofs, black as a crow's feathers and shiny as glass, would fit in the palm of your hand. She lifted her head. Her delicate ears twitched, her little black nose sniffed, and her great dark eyes looked with wonder at the world she had known for only a few days. Then she shivered and I knew she was afraid of me.

Slowly I backed away on tiptoe. The fawn, no longer frightened, laid down her head and closed her eyes. Although I was only a few steps from her, all I could see was the black tip of her nose, her long eyelashes, and her shiny black hoofs. I tiptoed

farther away and looked closely at the place where
she was lying, but I could not see her at all. The
most beautiful of all the forest creatures was
hidden from me by her marvelous camouflage.

13

The Beautiful Blue Jay

It is very cold in my woods now. Frost trims my windowpanes with patterns that look like flowers and ferns. Everywhere the snow is deep and there is no sound. Suddenly the silence runs away before the noisiest bird-talk you ever heard. The blue jays have come for lunch.

They wear beautiful violet-blue feathers, and have soft pale gray vests and lovely black and white trimming on their wings and tails. Their heads are crowned with fine feather crests, and their beaks and feet are black.

Mostly, blue jays eat seeds, fruit, nuts, and insects. They are very fond of acorns and sometimes they store them for winter food under leaves on the ground. Then they may forget all about the acorns, which sprout and grow into oak trees. The blue

They live all year around in the same place. In
summer you hear their lively, noisy voices in the
trees. In winter you can't miss seeing them dressed
in their bright blue feathers, as they flash across
the white snow.

The Woodchuck

By the side of my cabin there is a grassy place
like a tiny meadow, and here, under a big stone,
a woodchuck dug the front door to his underground
home. He pushed all the dirt from his tunnel
outside of the door and made a little round hill.
Now, when he comes outside, he stands on his little
hill and stretches as tall as he can and looks all
around for anything that might hurt him.

He is fat and his tail is short. He wears a
browny-gray coat, with a red front and sleeves. He
has pop eyes and his eyelids are almost always
half-shut. His front teeth are so big that they
stick out of his mouth. His legs are so stubby
that he waddles when he walks, and he can't run
very fast.

Because he lives under the ground and is fat like
a pig, he is often called groundhog. He is the only

animal who has a special day all his own—Groundhog Day, which is February second.

As soon as it gets chilly in the fall, he crawls into his underground house, stops up the doors with earth, and sleeps soundly all through the winter cold. People say that he comes outside the very first time on Groundhog Day. They say that if it is cloudy and he cannot see his shadow, he stays outside and it is spring; if the sun is shining and he sees his shadow, he is so scared that he runs right back into his house and it will not be spring for six more long weeks.

This is only a story, of course, because he isn't afraid of his shadow at all, but it is fun to wonder whether he will see his shadow on Groundhog Day.

My woodchuck loves to eat green things. He likes clover and dandelions and tender green grass, and he can eat enough to fill a big basket at one meal!

When he isn't eating, he goes straight back down into his house under the ground, where he is safe, and takes a nap.

Sometimes a woodchuck moves away and leaves his house empty. Then some other animal, who doesn't have strong claws and can't easily dig his own house, finds a fine home all ready for him. Lots of

rabbits live in homes that were dug by woodchucks.
Skunks and opossums and weasels and foxes like them,
too. The next time you are walking through an open
field, especially on a hillside, be on the lookout
for a woodchuck hole.

My woodchuck isn't very pretty or strong or brave,
but he is quiet and good-natured and helpful. He
would be a fine pet except that he is happier living
outside in his own house under the ground.

The Spring Peepers

In the earliest days of spring, when the snow has just melted and the new leaves are sprouting, I hear something saying, "Peep—peep—peep!" in the bushes near my cabin. It sounds like a bird—or maybe a fairy flute—but it really is a little tree frog called the spring peeper. As darkness falls hundreds of these frogs sing all at once, and then they sound like distant sleigh bells.

The peeper is so small that he could sit on an ordinary postage stamp. His cool skin is tan or brown. Darker markings form an X on his back, and others cross his arms and legs so that he looks as if he were wearing striped sleeves and stockings. On the tips of his long fingers and toes he has round sticky pads, with which he clings to stems and climbs into bushes and onto low tree branches.

When he sings, he takes a deep breath, closes his

mouth and nose, and forces air through a bag of skin at the front of his throat. Each time he peeps, this skin swells and forms a bubble that looks like a balloon and is almost half as big as the tiny frog. In between peeps, the bubble flattens against his throat. You would be lucky to see this frog, even with his call to guide you, because he is so cautious that he stops singing when he sees or hears anyone coming near him.

Soon after Mr. Peeper sings his spring song, Mrs. Peeper lays her eggs, one at a time or in clusters, attached to plant stems in pools of water. Instead of a shell, a covering of moist jelly protects each egg from drying out and spoiling if the water in the pool gets low.

Greenish tadpoles, with gold dots on their fat, round bodies and dark spots on their flat, wriggly tails, hatch from the eggs and swim in the pools. From mouth to tail-tip they are about once and a half as long as a postage stamp. Gradually they grow four little legs, while their tails get shorter and shorter. In about three months, their tails are gone and the tadpoles have turned into baby tree frogs, so small that *two* of them could sit on a stamp.

Spring peepers spend the summer in damp places, eating small insects. In the fall, they grow sleepy and burrow under mats of dead leaves, where they stay all winter. When spring again brings warm days and tasty insects, these wee frogs hop out from under the leaves.

If you listen closely, you will know when they are awake. You will hear them saying, "Peep—peep—peep—peep," perhaps even before you see a robin or a butterfly in your yard.

The Spotted Fawn

When new leaves are fluttering on the trees of my forest, and white flowers are scattered over the ground like leftover snow, Mrs. Deer's children are born. Deer babies are usually twins and they are called fawns.

One morning I looked out of the window at my garden and there, right by a patch of yellow lilies, stood a mother deer and her two fawns, who were no taller than the lilies. They wobbled on their thin legs and looked all around with their wide-open dark eyes. Their ears twisted this way and that, as they listened to bird songs and the little rustling sounds of the woods. Their coats were brown and covered with white spots. When Mrs. Deer saw me, she hurried her children out of sight behind the ferns and the honeysuckle bushes.

The little fawns can eat only their mother's milk.

When she goes to find leaves and twigs and buds to feed herself, she leaves her babies in a sheltered place, perhaps at the base of a big tree. You would think that the fawns would be in great danger from bears and bobcats, foxes and wolves and stray dogs, but nature has done two special things to keep them safe.

The fawns' spotted coats look just like the ground around them, where the sun shines in patches through the leaves. Animals who might want to eat the fawns cannot see them and cannot smell them either, because the fawns have almost no scent. If the fawns do just as mother deer has shown them and do not move, they are safe, because their enemies can walk right past them and never know they are there.

During the summer, Mrs. Deer teaches her growing children to find green things that are good to eat and she shows them the animals' trails through the forest. She gives them baths and gets burrs out of their soft fur by licking them all over with her long, pink tongue.

In the fall, they lose their spotted baby coats and grow gray or brown ones with white vests. Then they get the scent that tells other animals that they are in the forest, but they can leap so far and

so fast that they can almost always run away from
their enemies.

In another year, the young bucks will have grown
their first antlers and the young does will be as
tall and beautiful as their mother. Fawns grow up
just as human children do, only it doesn't take them
as long.

The River Otter

Mrs. Otter's home is in a hole in the bank of a stream or lake, or perhaps in a hollow tree. Sometimes she builds a round house of tall grass, but otters always live near water, because they spend most of their time swimming.

Everything about them is designed so that they can swim almost as well as a fish. Their long, slim bodies are covered with sleek, brown fur. Their strong, thick tails are narrowed to a point at the end. Their short legs are not very good for running on the ground, but their feet are webbed so that they can paddle through the water very fast.

Otter babies are born early in spring and, when they are five weeks old, their eyes open. Soon after, Mrs. Otter carries them on her back into the water and helps them learn to swim. Then she and her children, and even Mr. Otter, play tag and follow-the-leader, splashing and diving and ducking each other. They are the jolliest of all animals.

Sometimes a grownup plays all by himself, tossing a stone into the water and diving to see if he can catch it in his mouth before it gets to the bottom.

The otters' favorite game is sliding. There is an otter slide on the steep bank of the lake beside my cabin. One after another, the otters flop down flat, with their feet tucked back, and scoot headfirst into the lake. After they do this a few times, their wet bodies make the slide muddy and as slick as any in your playground. In the winter, the otters skid down the icy bank and end up topsy-turvy in the soft snow at the bottom.

Otters eat insects and water plants, snails, clams, and other small water creatures. Some people think they live on fish, but they eat very few because too many make them sick. When they hunt food in the wintertime, they go in and out of the holes in the ice and you'd think they would surely freeze. But they wear two natural overcoats: a layer of fat inside their skins and thick, soft fur outside.

Wolves and foxes would like to eat the otters, but they stay near the water so that they can pop in and swim away at any strange sound. Their beautiful fur

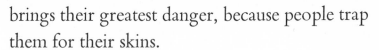

brings their greatest danger, because people trap
them for their skins.

Otter families are peaceful and loving. They lie
on the rocks in the warm summer sun. They swim and
play happily together all year. I hope that you
and your friends have as much fun playing together
as the otter children do.

The American Eagle

On July fourth, 1776, our country declared its independence. The men who formed our first government decided that the new nation needed a national emblem, and some years later the Great Seal of the United States was designed. Ask Mother to show you a one-dollar bill. On the back of it you will see the two sides of the Great Seal.

The bird on the front of the Great Seal is an American eagle, and you can see pictures and statues of him in many places—on government buildings like your post office, and in books.

He is very handsome, with dark brown wing and body feathers and white feathers in his tail and all over his head. Sometimes he is called the bald eagle, but he isn't bald at all. The white head feathers just make him look that way from a distance. His big wings spread eight feet. Ask someone to measure

this distance for you, so that you can see how very large the American eagle is. His yellow beak is hooked and his golden eyes are so keen that he can see his dinner even when it is miles away. Then he swoops down on his strong wings at a mile a minute to catch it.

He eats snakes, small animals, and fish. Sometimes he may steal a chicken, but he never carries off a human being, not even a baby, because his claws are not strong enough to lift anything that heavy. Often he eats meat that is left after animals have been killed by someone else, so none of the meat goes to waste.

The first thing that a new-hatched baby eagle sees is the sky, because eagles' nests are built on a cliff or a tall treetop. From this high point, Mr. and Mrs. Eagle can look far and wide for food or danger and, when the young eagles are big enough, they can fly from the nest into the high-up air.

Once I saw an American eagle in a cage at a zoo. His wings were clipped so that he could not fly and he looked very unhappy.

It is against the law to hurt American eagles, because most of them have been poisoned or shot. Not many are still alive, but sometimes I see them

flying over my woods. Just yesterday I saw one rise
from a treetop and go up in circles into the bright
sky. Up, up, up he went, until he was only a black
dot in the sunlight and then he went so high that I
could not see him any more.

That is the way I like to see the American eagle,
flying strong and free into the sunlight. After all,
he is the emblem of the United States, and we want
our country to be strong and free, too.

The Timber Wolf

You will probably never see a timber wolf except in a zoo because there are even fewer of them now than American eagles, and they live only in the wildest places, like the great forest around my cabin. Timber means big trees and the wolf is named for the trees of his forest.

A wolf looks just like a large dog, and he really is a wild dog that makes his own way in the wilderness. He listens with his pointed ears, sniffs for animal scents with his long nose, watches every movement with his slanted greenish eyes. His thick fur is gray or black or reddish-brown, and when he stretches his long, strong legs as he runs, his beautiful bushy tail flies out behind him like a banner.

In all the animal kingdom, there are no better parents than Mr. and Mrs. Wolf. The father hunts

night and day to bring food to the mother and her funny, fuzzy puppies. Wolves live in little family groups called packs and, sometimes, when two wolf mothers live close to each other, one mother will baby-sit with all the puppies while the other goes out for exercise.

When the babies begin to grow up, the parents teach them to hunt, because the youngsters must learn to catch their own food. Two or three wolves usually hunt together. They eat hares and other small animals, and they can even kill big animals, like moose and deer.

There is no good reason to hate wolves for this. They would die of hunger if they did not kill other animals. If some of these animals who eat plants were not killed, they would destroy the bushes and leaves. Then they would starve, too.

There isn't any reason to fear wolves, either. It is true that they are so quick and strong that they don't have to be afraid of other animals, but they run away from people as fast as they can.

Mr. and Mrs. Wolf stay in the hills during the summer while their puppies are small, but in the winter the whole family runs along the frozen lake in front of my cabin.

Sometimes they bark in big, gruff voices, and sometimes they howl so that it sounds as if they were singing. I like to see and hear them. They are part of my woods and I want them to be here always.

The Monarch Butterfly

In the fall, when the days grow short and cool, the birds get ready to fly south for the winter. Did you know that there is a fragile butterfly that does this, too? It is the orange and black monarch butterfly. So many monarchs gather together that bushes bend under their weight. Then, like a cloud of flowers, they rise into the air and fly thousands of miles to a warm place, where they can find food until the following spring.

If you look closely at a butterfly sitting on a flower you will see that he has a long tube tightly coiled beneath his big eyes. He uncoils this tube so that he can dip it into a flower and sip the sweet nectar.

Mrs. Monarch lays her eggs, which look like green drops of water, on the underside of the leaves of the milkweed plant, where they are sheltered from the rain and warmed by the sun. In about seven days, a small caterpillar hatches from each egg and begins to eat leaves.

He has white and yellow and black stripes running around his body, and two little horns at each end, with which he feels his way. This little caterpillar is a baby monarch butterfly! He grows very fast and sheds his skin several times. In a couple of weeks he is two inches long. Then he spins a silk thread from his mouth and uses this thread to fasten his tail to the underside of a leaf. During the next half hour, as he hangs there, a strange thing happens.

His body gets thicker and shorter and his skin splits and falls off. He has changed into a pupa, a partly grown-up butterfly, and is covered by a thin, tough case, shaped something like a tiny pear. The case in which a monarch pupa lives is green with little golden spots.

The pupa gradually changes into a butterfly, neatly folded inside the case. Then the butterfly begins to move and the case splits open.

The butterfly climbs outside, his wings all wet and broken-looking. As he slowly waves his wrinkled wings, they dry and straighten and take on the

beautiful colors of a grown-up butterfly.

If you find a pupa in its case, ask Mother or Dad
to cut the twig off carefully and take it home. If
it is not sick and does not get too hot it will open
in time.

It may be a monarch, some other kind of butterfly,
or a moth. Whatever it is, you will never forget
watching it come to life before your very eyes.

The Barred Owl

In October, my forest is all decorated for
Halloween, with bright orange leaves and long
black shadows under the trees. It looks as though it
might be full of funny witches and good-natured
spooks. No children live near enough to walk to my
door and say, "Tricks or treats!", and there are no
black cats in the woods, but on a dead tree limb in
my yard sits one of the most Halloweenish things in
the world—a big owl!

He is almost two feet tall. He blinks his big,
brown eyes at me and looks very wise and fat. His
body really is small and thin and he is mostly
fluffy feathers.

He is named the barred owl because crosswise
stripes, called bars, trim the upper part of his
vest. The lower part of it has handsome up-and-down
stripes, and his back and wings and tail are patterned

with gray and brown and white. When he sits quietly, you can hardly see him, because his feathers are the color of the branches around him.

His eyes are half-closed and you would think he was asleep, but he's watching the ground for a mouse, a weasel, or some other small animal. If he sees one, he will spread his wings almost as wide as you can stretch your arms, and fly down to catch his dinner. He has special, soft feathers on the edges of his wings so that he makes no sound when he flies. This helps him hunt, because the creature he wants cannot hear him coming.

The barred owl is very important in my forest, where there are many small animals that eat seeds. His job is to eat some of these animals, so that all the seeds will not be destroyed. Then the ones that are left will grow into green plants next summer.

A person does not often get to see an owl, because owls usually hunt at night. They have special eyes for seeing in the dark and they can hear the slightest sound. I know when the big barred owl is near my cabin, even when I don't see him, because he hoots very loudly and it sounds as if he were saying, "Who cooks for you? Who cooks for you-all?"

Sometimes several barred owls sit high in the

trees and talk to each other. They hoot and hiss, chuckle and grunt and cackle, all in their own owl language.

Perhaps when you are in the country you may hear an owl saying something that sounds like "Who? Who? Who?" But, of course, only another owl knows what he really means.

The Black Bears

One afternoon last summer I heard a lot of noise in my yard. My pet hen was cackling and something else was saying, "Whufff! Whufff! Whufff!"

I looked out and saw two baby bears, with black fur coats, big round ears, and pointed brown noses. They didn't know whether my hen was dangerous or not, so they climbed a tree. They held tight to the bark with their claws and peeked around the tree trunk.

Suddenly the big mother bear ran into the yard from the woods. When she stood up on her hind legs, she was taller than a man! The little bears knew they would be safe with mother, so they slid backward down the tree trunk and followed her to a blueberry patch, where they ate and ate.

Baby bears are almost always hungry. Mother bear will tear open a rotten log with her strong claws, so that her babies can lick up the ants that live

in the wood. She teaches them to sit beside a stream and catch a fish with a quick flash of a paw. She shows them where to find trees that the bees have filled with honey, and how to lift stones and eat insects that hide underneath. If people go camping and forget to put away their bacon, the bears smell it—and eat that, too.

When the little bears are not eating, they take baths in ponds or brooks, and comb their fur smooth with their claws. Sometimes they walk along the sunny road, or run through the shady forest paths, just for fun. Sometimes they see a papa bear, wandering around by himself.

In the fall, when the cold winds come and the leaves turn brown, the bears eat even more than usual. When they are fat and their fur coats are thick and shiny, they find a cave or hollow stump and go to sleep inside it. They don't sleep as soundly as the peepers and woodchucks. Sometimes they even wake up for a little while, but they live on their own fat and don't need to eat. Each big bear has his own place, and I'm sure my two little bears are curled up together. They will rest there, cozy and warm, until the snow melts again in the spring.

Then the little bears will be big enough to take care of themselves. This is a good thing, because mother bear will have new babies when she wakes up and comes out of her cave.

If you go on vacation in the deep woods next summer, maybe you will see some bears, walking along a road or hunting for a jam jar or a piece of bread in a garbage dump. Maybe you have already seen them in your zoo, sitting up and begging for popcorn. They are lots of fun to watch, but you must never tease them or go close to them, because teasing is cruel, and bears are too big and strong to play with.

The Caribou

In the faraway lands near the North Pole live the caribou, big cousins of the gentle deer who stay near my cabin. Mr. Caribou wears a thick, brown coat, with a fluffy, snow-white mane around his shoulders and down over his chest. His head is crowned with large and graceful antlers. Mrs. Caribou has a smaller mane and antlers. Their long-legged babies do not have any.

Their country is called The Barrens because it is so cold that no bushes or trees can grow there—only hardy mosses and other small plants.

The caribou are named from an Indian word that means "someone who shovels," because they shovel the snow with their big hoofs to find the tiny plants that they eat. Their full name is the barren-grounds caribou.

You might think that their bare country is ugly,

but it is a place of strange and wonderful things. In midsummer, the sun shines all day and all night, and its warmth melts the snow. Then masses of bright-colored flowers cover the earth like a sweet-smelling carpet. In midwinter, the sun does not rise high enough to be seen and it is dark all the time. Overhead the sky is filled with the Northern Lights, red, green and white, that sometimes wave like searchlights or hang like curtains. Sometimes they form arches like silver rainbows.

Long ago, many great herds of caribou trotted across The Barrens. Eskimos killed a few of them with arrows and spears, to eat their meat and make warm clothing and strong leather from their skins. Wolves followed the herds and ate the weak ones, and the sick. Then men came with guns. In the treeless land, there was no place where the caribou could hide, so thousands of them were shot. Now only a few herds are left in all their wide lands.

When your great-grandfather was a little boy, woodland caribou lived in the forest where I live now. They ate plants that grew under the big Christmas trees. When many of these trees were cut down to make boards and paper, these caribou moved

to other woodlands where they could find proper
food. Not long ago, someone told me a few of them
have returned and are living not far from my cabin.
Someday I may look out and see one at my doorstep.

In the far-north part of Europe, people have tamed
the barren-grounds caribou and hitch them up like
horses to pull sleighs. It may be a surprise to
learn that these tame caribou are old friends of
ours.

Their other name is reindeer, and everybody knows
that when Santa Claus does not come by plane or
automobile, his sleigh is pulled straight from the
North Pole by his own reindeer team!

Winter Sleep

If you could look out of my cabin window in wintertime, you would think that the birds and animals had gathered to have a party in the snow.

Chickadees pick up bits of suet. Blue jays call "jay-jay-jay!" to each other. Squirrels chatter as they eat corn, and lovely deer stand quietly, cleaning their fur with their tongues. But many of my animal friends are not here.

What has become of the frogs and toads? Where did my bears and chipmunks go? Where are the skunks and woodchucks, and other friends who come to my yard in summer?

They are asleep—that's where.

In the chilly autumn, the insects die, and the berries and leaves turn red and yellow and fall onto the ground. Then the animals who eat these things get ready to sleep until warm weather comes back and there is food for them again. I have already told you about the spring peepers, the woodchucks, and the bears. Now I will tell you about some of the others.

The spotted green frogs that hop through the grass snuggle into hollows under leaves or stones, and the sleepy-looking brown toads dig holes in the earth. They close their eyes and gradually get colder and colder. They hardly breathe and their little hearts beat very slowly. If you were to pick one of them up, you would think that he was dead, but he is only resting in the very deep sleep called hibernation.

The little jumping mice sleep almost as soundly as the frogs and toads.

These pretty creatures hop about like wee kangaroos in the summer, and make nests of leaves and hair to keep the cold away while they hibernate.

The chipmunks do not sleep as soundly. All summer they store seeds and nuts in their underground homes. When fall comes they have enough food to last until spring, and in they go, to doze and wake up, eat a little, then maybe sleep some more.

The skunks spend most of the winter in their burrows under the ground, but sometimes, when there is a sunny day that is not too cold, they come out for a walk. The raccoons stay up most of the winter, only dozing in their tree holes when it is very cold.

I watch for my sleepy friends when it begins to get warm. Sure enough, before all the snow has gone, the chipmunks are scurrying around in the sun. Then the bears come walking along the trails and the woodchucks sit up in front of their burrows. The peepers peep and the frogs croak and the toads sing in the rain. No matter how long the winter, I know that when spring comes my sleeping friends will wake up and come back to my doorstep.